Auld Scottish Grannies' Remedies

A Haggis A Day Keeps The Doctor Away

Betty Kirkpatrick

Crombie Jardine
PUBLISHING LIMITED

Unit 17, 196 Rose Street, Edinburgh EH2 4AT
www.crombiejardine.com

This edition was first published by Crombie Jardine
Publishing Limited in 2005

ISBN 1-905102-06-2

Designed by www.mrstiffy.co.uk
Printed and bound in the United Kingdom by
William Clowes, Beccles, Suffolk

DISCLAIMER!

Although the remedies in this book were once favoured by grannies, this is essentially a humorous work, not a medical one, and its recommendations should not be followed. Anyone needing medical attention should always consult a doctor.

www.crombiejardine.com

CONTENTS

MODERN
SCOTS GRANNY

In Scotland today, Granny is still an important, much-loved person in many families. When things go wrong in a Scots child's life, it is still often a case of Granny to the rescue.

Grannies still give the most comforting cuddles to counteract the many disasters of modern childhood, such as skinned knees, difficult sums, lost pocket money or failure to get the toy-of-the-year for Christmas.

SCOTS GRANNY'S SECRET WEAPON

A bag of sweeties is still a major part of Scots Granny's rescue kit. Nowadays these, known in England simply as sweets, are likely to be shop-bought, whereas formerly Scots grannies might well have kept a hoard of home-made treats, such as tablet (a mouth-watering, if cavity-inducing, delicacy made with condensed milk) or tooth-breaking treacle toffee. Of course, grannies of yesteryear did rely on one shop-bought treat as a remedy for childhood illness. This was the pan

drop, a kind of hard, smooth
peppermint sweet intended to be
sucked slowly.

A CHANGE OF IMAGE

Loved as they are, Scots grannies
are not what they once were.
For a start, they have
shed the traditional
image of a granny. The
little white-haired
lady, clad in floor-
length, shapeless
black and sitting
by an open fire

stirring a pot or knitting a sock, is no more. Today's Scots Granny is more likely to be sporting the best modern gear she can afford and have had her hair tinted to a hue of her choice at the local hairdresser. She will have swapped the pot on the open fire for a microwave oven and may well have given up sock-knitting in favour of paid employment.

But there has been a price to
pay for all this progress and
that price is a loss of power.
True, Scots Granny has retained
some of this. She was, after
all, the person who told her

grandchildren's parents what to do – and possibly still does – and that makes her grandchildren view her with awe as well as love. Modern Scots Granny, however, simply does not play the pivotal family role that her predecessors did.

"Learn young, learn fair, learn old, learn more."
Scottish proverb

SCOTS GRANNY OF YESTERYEAR

Scots grannies of previous generations played many roles. They often performed many of the household tasks, without any labour-saving devices, especially when the younger women

were pregnant
or looking
after young
children. Most
importantly,
they were the
guardians, and
often executors,
of the family
traditional
remedies.

These were times when medical help might be far away and unaffordable. Thus Granny was often doctor and nurse as well as head cook and bottle-washer. In order to perform her medical role, auld Scots Granny, like grannies of the time all over the world, relied heavily on everyday things around her. In her case, however – for don't forget she was a Celt – these were often interspersed with a good deal of superstition and regard for the supernatural.

THE BIRTH OF GRANDCHILDREN

The role of auld Scots Granny
in the lives of her grandchildren
sometimes began even before
they were conceived.
In this modern
age there are many
aids to fertility,
but only a few
decades ago, there

was only Granny and her like. She had several pieces of advice for couples who experienced problems in conceiving.

One was that the woman of the couple rub herself against a woman who was pregnant. Another was that the couple carry out their conception routine out of doors, rather than in the comfort of their bedroom. There was something about lying on the ground that was meant to increase the chances of conception, particularly if this took place under a tree.

When the grandchild was duly conceived and born, auld Scots Granny used to carry out rather a strange remedy for a circumstance that might befall the grandchild when he/she grew up. In order to prevent the child from remaining unmarried or childless, when

he/she reached adulthood,
Granny would wrap a male child
in his mother's petticoats, or a
female child in her father's shirt.

GRANNY'S BATTLE
WITH THE FAIRIES

Auld Scots Granny, like other grannies, would have had a lot of extra duties to perform when there had been a new birth in the house, but her extra work involved an unusual element. She had to safeguard mother and child against the fairy folk. In many parts of Scotland, as in Ireland, people, until

comparatively recently, had a
strong belief in the existence of
these. Furthermore, the fairy
folk whom auld Scots Granny

had in mind were not the delicate, pretty little harmless creatures whom people might envisage dancing in a ring at the foot of their gardens.

No, these fairies were considered to be very powerful and malevolent.

Their power was particularly feared at times of childbirth, because it was believed that the fairies might try to carry off the woman who had just given birth, or the child who had just been born and was as yet unbaptized. Part of the reason for this concern was that the fairies were particularly fond of human milk.

"Luck never gives; it only lends."
Scottish proverb

Fairy Deterrents

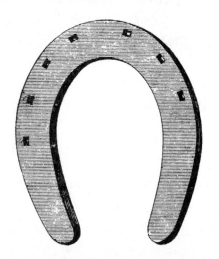

 Auld Scottish
grannies felt
that they had
to call on
all of their
Granny wiles
to thwart the devious fairies,
and these wiles took all shapes
and forms. Fife Granny, for
example, thought that a lucky
horseshoe hung at the fireside
would do the trick. Other
grannies might put an old shoe

on the fire so that it would make a lot of smoke and ward off the fairies. Several Scots grannies would take long-term action against supernatural beings, such as witches and fairies, by planting a rowan tree (also known as a mountain ash) in the front garden or by the front door, as traditionally this was thought to keep the evil ones at bay.

In some parts of Scotland, such as Aberdeenshire or Kincardineshire, Granny pinned a silver brooch in the shape of a heart, known as a witch-brooch, to a child's underclothes when he/she was first dressed. This was then pinned on each successive set of clothes until the child was quite old. It was intended to keep the child safe not only from witches

but also from fairies
and from evil in general.
Another possible witch deterrent
involved wrapping a piece of
red worsted material around
the child's wrist.

There were several other fairy
deterrents on which Granny
insisted when a child was
young. If a child's nappies were
left outside to dry or air, they
must be taken in before sunset
– otherwise, the fairies might
gather them up and use them
to bring harm to the child. Even
more harm might be done if
the fairies got hold of any hair
or nail-clippings from the baby.
Thus Granny saw to it that

such hair was burnt. The nail clippings were either burnt or swallowed by the baby's mother. She would have been advised by Granny to bite the baby's nails, rather than cut them, to prevent accidental loss.

"A woman conceals what she knows not."
Scottish proverb

MORE FAIRY DETERRENTS

Auld Scots Granny's battle against the fairies was a tough one and some of her strategies needed more drastic action than others. Highland Granny might arrange for a row of iron nails to be hammered into the board at the front of the bed so that the fairies were physically warded off. Alternatively, she might sprinkle the door posts with human urine. This can't have been very pleasant for the inhabitants of the house, but the smell of human urine was apparently detested by fairy folk and therefore likely to keep them out.

Meanwhile, in the North-East of Scotland, Granny might be found placing a bible and some kind of food – often a piece of bread and a chunk of cheese, or a biscuit – under the pillow

of the woman
who had just
given birth, and
saying a prayer
urging God to keep her and her
baby safe. Alternatively, a piece
of fir-wood might be lit like a
candle and either carried three
times right around the bed or
whirled three times around the
heads of the mother and baby.
Three, like nine, was considered
a magical number.

In several parts of Scotland, Granny might use a garment of the baby's father to frighten the fairies away. Sometimes a pair of his trousers was hung at the foot of the bed in which mother and baby slept; sometimes one of his shirts would be used to wrap the newborn baby in.

CHANGELINGS

Fear of the fairies was always increased when there was a newborn child in the house, because it was believed that the fairies would try to spirit it away, leaving one of their own in its place. Such a fairy baby was known as a changeling, and it would be the fate of the family whose baby was stolen to have to rear this stranger.

If either Scots or Irish Granny

had a suspicion
that the baby in
its mother's
bed was not
the original
baby, but a changeling, she
might take rather drastic
action. Her suspicions might,
for example, have been aroused
by the fact that the baby seemed
to be crying excessively and
in what was thought to be an
unnatural way.

If Granny decided that there
was a possibility that the baby
in the cot was a changeling she
considered that it was time for
her to 'put on the girdle'. The
girdle, or griddle, was the flat
circular iron pan on which
Granny cooked her pancakes,
scones and oatcakes and this

was put on the fire as though
Granny were about to start
baking. The child whose fairy
origins were suspected was then
held very near the fire. If the
child was indeed a changeling,
it would, supposedly, go right

up the chimney and the real child would return home by the same route. The purpose of the griddle, apparently, was to catch the real child and so prevent it from being burned by the flames of the fire. Unfortunately, this was a dangerous test and casualties were not unknown.

WARDING OFF BAD LUCK

Being taken by the fairies was the worst piece of luck that could befall a child, but auld Scots Granny also tried to ensure that no ill luck of any kind would befall her grandchild. Some of Granny's rules about ill luck were more curious than others.

Rather an odd one forbade

people from carrying newborn
children downstairs before they
were carried upstairs – perhaps
this had something to do with
heaven and hell. In any case,
it was not always easy to bring
about this particular feat, unless
the house in which the baby
was born had several floors.
However, Scots Granny was
nothing if not ingenious and,
in the absence of stairs, either
Granny herself or the midwife,

known as the howdie, climbed
on a chair or box to fulfil the
good-luck requirement.

Granny also had to take
care that the child did not
unwittingly invite bad luck
for itself. She stipulated that
mirrors should be kept away
from young children for as long
as possible. This was not just
because the child might break

it and bring him/herself seven years of bad luck – for auld Scots Granny was as aware of this superstition as were grannies in other parts of the world – but also because Granny believed that exceptionally bad luck would befall a child who looked in the mirror before they had acquired teeth.

This was an especially morbid superstition, since this particular piece of bad luck

might well mean that the child
would die before reaching the
age of five years old.

Scarcely less morbid was
Granny's suggestion that
it was unlucky for a child of
six weeks or so to watch smoke
going up the chimney. The
child might never reach its first
birthday if it did.

THe Lucky cauL

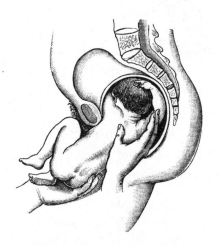

So far it might seem that auld Scots Granny with all her ill-luck remedies was a bit of a pessimist. However, good luck could befall children as well as bad, and lucky indeed was the child who was born with a caul. This was the belief of some other grannies as well, particularly Irish Granny. Indeed, the superstition seems to have been worldwide and is meant to be the origin of the French expression *être né coiffé* which means to be born lucky, or, as we say in English, to be born with a silver spoon in one's mouth. The literal translation of the French is to be born with something on one's head, probably a lucky caul.

The caul is a name given to
the membrane surrounding
the amniotic fluid in the

womb and
sometimes
a piece of
this attaches
to the baby,
particularly
to the baby's
head, during
the birth
process. Auld

Scots Granny, of course, had no control over whether any of her grandchildren would have the luck to be born with a caul, but she could preserve it carefully. If the caul should be lost or destroyed, it was thought that the child who had been born with it would pine or even die.

The caul was thought not only to bring the child general good

luck, but also to prevent his/her death by drowning. This capacity extended beyond the child born with a caul. Scots grannies who lived by the sea, as in parts of Fife, would give pieces of the cherished caul to family fishermen as they set out on potentially dangerous voyages.

THE 'GIFT'

Highland Granny believed implicitly that certain people were born with the gift to see into the future. Indeed, this was sometimes called having the 'Gift' or having the 'second sight'. Children who were born with a caul were, in Granny's opinion, particularly likely to have the second sight and they were encouraged by her to develop the gift.

The seventh son of a seventh son, or even the seventh child of a seventh child was also so blessed, in Granny's opinion.

"One for sorrow, two for joy, three for a girl, four for a boy, five for silver, six for gold and seven for a secret that must never be told."
Scottish proverb

GRANNY'S MEDICAL WARNINGS

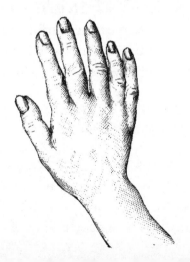

As her grandchildren grew up, auld Scots Granny had medical remedies to pass on to them and sometimes these took the form of dire warnings. Her philosophy was that prevention was better than cure.

She warned, for example, not to get even the slightest of injuries near the heart, as these were likely to cause death. Such a fate

 was also liable to befall anyone who received even a slight scratch in the area of that other vital point, the jugular vein. What anxiety must have been suffered by someone absent-mindedly scratching his/her neck with sharp nails!

Hiccups are often received with
amusement by those other than
the sufferer. Auld Scots Granny,
however, took the condition
extremely seriously. Hiccups

were to be avoided at all costs, or cured as soon as possible, since Granny was of the opinion that these were caused by a nerve in the heart and that a drop of blood left the heart with every hiccup. This must have been a terrifying thought for anyone – particularly children – prone to attacks of hiccups.

Eyeteeth – the canine teeth
located on each side of the upper
jaw below the eyes – were not to
be extracted, however painful.
According to Scots Granny,
any pain would just have to
be endured, as pulling out an
eyetooth might well result in
significant damage being done
to the eyesight.

Granny's warnings were also extended to the thumb. It should be kept safe from injury as much as possible, although, given its position, this must have been difficult. Injury to it, according to Granny, would cause lockjaw, more formally known as tetanus and a serious condition. Nowadays, however, tetanus injections have greatly reduced our dread of it.

SHINGLES

Such warnings issued by Scots
Granny were bad enough when
it was possible, however difficult,
to take note of them and act
accordingly. But some of them
were terrible predictions rather
than warnings of situations
that could be prevented. After
all, some situations were beyond
human control.

Take Scots Granny's terrible warning about shingles, for example. This is a painful condition that can cause a rash on the trunk and Granny darkly predicted that the condition would prove fatal if the shingles rash should meet in the middle. Picture the anxiety of the patient, who probably examined the rash every 10 minutes to see if there was any sign of this fatal meeting occurring!

WASHING

One of Scots Granny's warnings concerned personal hygiene, but it was not the kind of admonition you might expect from someone so highly respected. Granny's advice was not to wash too much, or it might cause weakness of the limbs and general debility. Menstruating women, in particular, were advised against washing extensively for the duration of their periods, and

this advice also applied to
their underwear and bed linen.
Shame on Granny! But she
thought it was for the best.

"They that smell least, smell best."
Scottish proverb

FOOD AND DRINK

Scots Granny seems to have had an aversion to water for drinking as well as water for washing. It was her advice that water should not be taken by an ill person, especially if the patient was feverish. Nor should it be consumed by someone who had just given birth. Granny's advice was thus completely out of step with the advice often given today – to drink as much water as possible, especially when you are ill. However, it may well have been a reasonable precaution in an age when water purity was far less certain.

It was Granny's belief also that food as well as water should be given sparingly in cases of fever.

'Feed a cold and starve a fever' was one of her favourite sayings and, indeed, this particular philosophy was popular in other cases. As far as the common cold and other diseases were concerned, Granny's patients were luckier and they would be given nourishing food, although she often worried that the food might strengthen the disease as well as the patient's system.

To be fair to Granny, her medical intervention did not only take the form of preventive warnings. When it came to medical matters, she was very much hands-on. Just as she fought the fairies and ill luck, she fought a constant battle against any injuries and disease that might occur in her large family.

"Better wait on the cook than the doctor."
Scottish proverb

whooping cough remedies

Some conditions were more recalcitrant than others and warranted a battery of Granny remedies. One such condition was whooping cough. In these modern days of vaccination programmes, it is no longer such a problem, unless the parents have elected not to have their child vaccinated. At worst, most children might now get a mild form of whooping cough, but in earlier days it was a common

and most distressing, not to
mention sometimes dangerous,
disorder. Known in Scots as
'kink-hoast', it was passed from
child to child by one 'getting
the smit' from another. In other
words it was infectious.

A CHANGE OF AIR

One of Scots Granny's simpler remedies was a change of air. This did not, necessarily, involve a great deal of time, distance or money. A trip of a few miles would do, just enough to convince Scots Granny – often, in this case, Fife Granny – that the air being breathed by the child was somehow different.

A particular form of air was also important in another of Scots Granny's cures for

whooping cough. The child
might be taken to a limekiln, a
gasworks or even down a pit, as
in parts of Fife, to breathe in the
air of the particular location.

Alternatively, the child might be taken to a place where a road was being mended and urged to breathe in the smell of the tar. More strangely, the child might be held over a freshly dug hole and told to breathe in the smell of the earth.

"Evening oats are good morning father."
Scottish proverb

Donkeys and White Horses

Some of Scots Granny's
remedies for whooping cough
demonstrate her allegiance
to the supernatural or to
superstition. For example,
she might advise that a child
suffering from the condition be
passed under a donkey, possibly
because the donkey was thought
to have unusual powers from its
association with Christ.

Yet another of Granny's
decidedly strange whooping
cough cures also involved a four-
legged beast of burden. This
time it was a horse, and a white
horse at that – or occasionally
a piebald one. The wretched
young patient, who undoubtedly
would have been better off in
bed, was carried around, at
Granny's insistence, until they
met a man on a white horse.
The said man, who presumably

could have taken a considerable time to appear, was then asked to recommend a good cure for whooping cough. Whatever he suggested must be carried out to the letter, Granny decreed, although if the man on the white horse was just idly riding by, he must have been quite taken aback at the request.

This curious remedy was
not unique to Scots Granny.
Across the Irish Sea, Irish
Granny, particularly if she lived
in County Clare or County
Longford, was also to be found

urging people to seek out men on white horses and carry out their recommendations as to whooping cough cures. It has been speculated that the origin of the supposed cure might lie in the fact that the early doctors might have commonly ridden on white horses, but no one really knows.

SHARING SURNAMES

There is also a connection
between Scots Granny and Irish
Granny in relation to another
prescribed Granny cure for
whooping cough. In Scotland
Granny recommended that a
remedy might be effected if
the whooping cough sufferer
was given bread and milk by
a woman whose maiden and
married surnames were the
same. In Ireland there were
various cures throughout the

country based
on a similar idea.
For example, in
County Leitrim it was common
for Irish Granny to send a
messenger to a husband and
wife who had shared a surname
before marriage, as well as after,
and ask them to give Granny's
messenger the first and last
piece of their breakfasts. This
was then given to the whooping
cough patient.

TRANSFERENCE

Transference was a concept that
played a part in cures in many
parts of the world and it was
also the basis of some of Scots
Granny's cures, demonstrating
the universality of some of
her ideas. The idea behind
transference cures, although
Scots Granny would not have
described them so grandly,
was that the disease should
be passed on to someone or
something else and so leave the

original sufferer free of it.

In the case of Scots Granny and whooping cough, a transference cure might take the form of placing a live spider in a bag round the patient's neck. The hope was that the illness would pass to the spider which would then die and bring the cure to a successful conclusion. An even more bizarre transference

cure, occasionally practised by
Scots Granny, involved getting
the whooping cough patient
to cough into a live fish or
frog. The creature was then
placed back in the water in the

hope that it would catch the infection, die, and thus effect a cure.

I have chosen to dwell so long on whooping cough cures because they demonstrate both the considerable range and diversity of Scots Granny's remedies – not to mention the strangeness of several – and their connections with other countries.

ꙍORꙂS

In days when personal hygiene was not taken as seriously as it is today, many of auld Scots Granny's brood were apt to suffer from an infestation of intestinal worms. As you can imagine, her remedies were much unlike today's cures purchased at the chemist. One of these involved getting the sufferer to chew a piece of bread and then spit this out before taking a drink of whisky. Apparently Granny reckoned that the worms would open their mouths to consume the bread and then be drowned in the whisky. It is not known how the worms felt about such a death!

BED-WETTING

Granny is bound to have regarded bed-wetting as a tiresome failing, given that it would increase the volume of the family wash, and some of her efforts to prevent it were rather drastic. For example, Fife Granny sometimes took to boiling a mouse in water and then giving the bed-wetter a tablespoon of the resultant liquid three times a day. Alternatively, she might cut the head off the mouse, roast it, pulverize it and give the powder to the child. Let us hope that the child did not know the ingredients of Granny's remedy or he/she would be likely to wet the bed in sheer terror at the thought of the cure!

Scots Granny had also other methods of being tough on bed-wetters. The child was sometimes made by her to drink his/her own urine, or to take porridge which had been mixed with some of this. Perhaps Scots Granny was of the school of thought that thinks that you have to be cruel to be kind!

TOOTHACHE

It was an ancient belief, and one that went on being fashionable for a very long time, that toothache was caused not by overindulging in sweet, sugary things, but by somehow having got a worm in the tooth. The hole in the tooth was taken as evidence of the worm's presence. Auld Scots Granny's cure for a worm in the tooth that was causing so much pain was to advise the sufferer to sniff salt

up the nose or to smoke tobacco until he/she was sick.

A much more acceptable cure was whisky soaked in a plug of cotton wool and applied to the tooth. As you might expect, this was much used both by Scots and Irish Granny, although Scots Granny had a saying which showed that she generally encouraged the drinking of whisky rather than the external application of it. This was 'let the sau sink to the sair', translated literally as 'let the salve sink to the sore place', but more loosely translated as 'drink the whisky rather than rubbing it in'. I'm sure that this was one of Scots Granny's suggestions that was well and truly heeded!

It is interesting to note that some Australian grannies also used whisky as a toothache cure, but they did not advise drinking it. Instead, they dipped a small piece of brown paper in whisky, sprinkled this with pepper, applied it to the face over the spot where the pain was, and covered it with a flannel bandage.

poULTICES

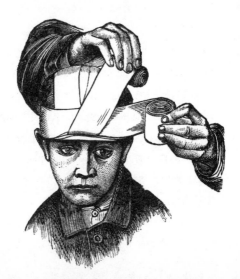

Scots Granny was a great believer in the healing power of poultices. These usually consisted of a hot semi-liquid substance spread on a piece of cloth, a piece of brown paper or something similar – such as a cabbage leaf – and applied to the skin. Granny thought that they were excellent at drawing out whatever was causing the problem and she used them, for example, to draw boils. Poultices were also used by Granny on the chest to relieve respiratory conditions and on swollen joints to soothe them.

The substances that granny used varied quite a bit, but her repertoire included carrots, turnips, cabbage, bread, and a mixture of sugar and soap, to name but a few. A whitlow, a painful area of inflammation around the side of a fingernail, demanded the use of a poultice made either from chopped leeks, chewed tobacco leaf, or soap and sugar.

"Lang fasting hains nae meat."
Scottish proverb

BLEEDING

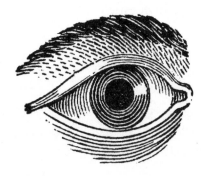

Scots Granny also often had accidents to contend with, as well as illnesses. Many of these resulted in loss of blood and again Scots Granny had more than one remedy to hand.

Like English Granny, and indeed several other grannies, she used cobwebs to stop bleeding. It was fortunate that housewives were not then as houseproud as they are now. Finding a spider's web today might be tricky!

Occasionally Granny would
try a like-to-like treatment
when bleeding was involved.
Thus she might wrap a piece
of red cloth round the part that
was bleeding in the belief
that the red material might
stop the red blood.

She used the same idea when
she tied a baby's umbilical cord
with red cord to prevent it from
bleeding, or placed a piece of red
cloth at the foot of a childbirth

bed so as to prevent any post-labour haemorrhaging.

Scots Granny feared that the soul might slip away from the body if there was significant blood loss. In order to avoid such a calamity she would tie a piece of thread to the wounded person's thumb in an effort to keep body and soul together.

NETTLE STINGS

Just as Scots Granny shared a blood-staunching remedy with grannies from other countries, so she shared a remedy for nettle stings. The standard traditional cure throughout Great Britain and Ireland was the application of dock leaves. Handily, these often grow besides nettles. The cure was thought to be all the more effective if a bit of spit was added to the dock leaf.

FASTING SPIT

Mention of spit leads me to another strange remedy which was part of Scots Granny's repertoire. Once again, it was also common in several other parts of the world, including Ireland.

The remedy was known as 'fasting spit' or 'fasting spittle', being either the saliva of someone who has been fasting for a considerable time, or the saliva of someone who has not had anything to eat or drink that day. Fasting spittle was regarded universally as a defence against evil and, by extension, it was also used against disease.

Scots Granny recommended rubbing it both on warts and sore eyes.

FAITH

As you will see, auld Scots Granny had many remedies which she hoped would keep her family in good health. Some of these required administering either three or nine times, both numbers having a mystical significance in Granny's culture, as in others.

As with other folk remedies, many of Granny's cures required an element of faith, but that was no problem.

All the family had implicit faith in auld Scots Granny.